T0279516

The Signature Series
048 of 100

Praise for *Bledsoe*

William Wright's haunting new volume, Bledsoe, is a book-length, paean-lament, chiseled into thirty-seven sections of truncated supple couplets. It is the odyssey of Durant Bledsoe, a mute Appalachian savant-seer, ultimately and literally orphaned, but also remanded to wander untended in the weir of his own preternatural psyche. Wright's language, difficult to dub because it is so inspiring, comes from that other inscrutable place as well—by turns like gentle rain, but more often like Gatling gun fire, a fusillade or linguistic and aural sophistication that is truly fascinating. The entire poem is fever dream-like, mythic, yet girded by searing narrative rooted in, of all places, Yancy County, North Carolina—which rarifies this luminous book all the more.

—Joseph Bathanti, Author of ***Land of Amnesia*** and ***Restoring Sacred Art***

Bledsoe reads like a poem by Cormac McCarthy. In startling, vivid lyrics, Bledsoe unfolds as an intense drama of affliction and the mystery of consciousness and time, of curse and exorcism, of nightmare and the rejuvenating power of nature in cycles of growth and decay. Wight has created his own haunted world, with different voices, interior voices. Sometimes a prayer, sometimes a scream, sometimes a folksong, the poem is a narrative of care giving, devotion, violence, and love. You will not soon forget it.

—Robert Morgan, Author of ***Gap Creek*** and ***Terroir***

William Wright's Bledsoe has the ambition of an extended narrative reminiscent of the down-home, home-sung lyrics or Claudia Emerson's Pinion. Bledsoe's style, however, is more sparse and hungry, the words snapping with the crispness of a cold apple bitten into. This "unearthed gospel" of sorrow and loss in the rural south is seething with life and memorable language, sculpting a landscape where "insects chisel the night to a point," which is exactly what Wright does, making radiance of darkness and finding dignity in affliction.

—R.T. Smith, Editor of ***Shenandoah***

Through language wound tight as baling wire, Wright conjures Bledsoe out of the backwoods and into our world where he lodges like a burr in our imagination. Rarely has a contemporary poetic voice achieved the incantatory with such skill, echoes of Cormac McCarthy's word-hoard pulsing throughout! Wright's couplets stride, stagger, and rage, burning Bledsoe's inner and outer landscapes like a cattle brand into our memory. I can imagine a medieval skald or jongleur singing this poem around a fire, his listeners' faces rapt with listening, as any reader of Bledsoe will be, lost in the spell cast by this powerful poem.

—Kathryn Stripling Byer, Author of ***Coming to Rest*** and ***Wildwood Flower***

Bledsoe

LIMITED EDITION

Printed and Bound in the United States of America
First Edition Copyright: 2011

Library of Congress Cataloging-in-Publication Data
is on file at the Library of Congress, Washington, DC

Published by TRP: The University Press of SHSU
Huntsville, Texas 77341
texasreviewpress.org

Bledsoe

A Poem

William Wright

TRP: The University Press of SHSU
Huntsville, Texas

To Jesse Graves

in empathy

Contents

A man goes far to find out what he is–
Death of the self in a long, tearless night,
All natural shapes blazing unnatural light.

Theodore Roethke

I. Behind the Brick Pits

Behind the brick pits
    of Yancey County Waterworks,

Durant Bledsoe wobbles
    out of sumac and bellwort,

grimaces pink-skinned
    at how the world spins, swings

to the right. Hobbles along
    the tree line from the braid

of sirens, the asphalt's linear
    prophecy, forehead super-

heated and scathed in the sweeping
    back and flay of limbs.

Gasping. Shame a char-smear
    on his ear. Sweat begins to rinse

that filth away. Hemorrhage-hot,
    dead center, the sun grinds

his muttering down to bare
    declaration, whine and howl:

Ain't no need to warsh, Mama,
    when I seen your blood the while.

Ain't no need to warsh
    when you're bald of mouth and eyes.

Smells of smolder, choking
    on panic with trees leaning in.

Mind-frayed, he turns to memory,
    images flashpoints of light

searing, the story unbolted
    and lucid, sparked by the flinty

dusk-kindling of insects. Car engines
    jeweled by distance, shining nearer.

2. Far Down in the Parched Hollows

Far down in the parched hollows
 of summertime, Bledsoe,

seven, woke paralyzed, reed-like
 on counterpane to crickets' blare.

Too hot to sleep, he forced his
 eyes to the shut window, stared.

Something lumbered his bones
 to lead weight, heaved down hard.

Night-shadows dappled
 the hickories as clouds chipped

away at the moonglow. He heard
 goats' bleat, mix and rut

around the hedge. Then, more
 heaviness: a bulk pressed down

like the roof's weight on his heart,
 sharp, raw, his blood made lacertilian.

The window an eye. The view
 of the yard smoke-stung

and quivering as though licked by heat
 of a fire Bledsoe could not see.

His gaze wormed by gray dream-fog
 yawning in from murk.

Clinched his eyes shut. Knew in that
 burning dark that something

breathed. In those eyelids' brain-
    made signs, he became

a lure to ghosts and seer
    of the other world, understood

then how the moon found him lodged
    cold in his own body, the window

his only lens. Knew the wisdom
    of movement in torpor,

minnows prodding rain-scalloped
    shores, each spine anchored

for the moment's purpose. Knew too
    soon that the oak is a chapel

through which owls shake and bow
    dark beams, leaf-light

patinas on the far wall. And what
    was the music that fell

on the grass out there, approaching
    in the shuttered dark?

Susurrus. Leaves crackling like fire,
    low-lying sentience, muscled

kindling to split the earth-mat.
    Silence. He realized

he must look with his mind halved,
    a blue apple. Opened his eyes

to slits, his temples dread-wet–
    Serpents black and brown

writhed around the sill, thrashed
    to gain traction up the glass.

A yellow snake, king-father,
uncoiled girth from his shadow

kin as though from the dark gathering
of first Creation, first radiance.

Became the center Bledsoe's
revelation, the torsional answer

to thrash in that fear. The child warred
to shunt his body, to unlatch voice

until he heard himself croak out,
yell for mother, the sound

alien, thrown strange across
the house to his parents'

bedroom where she bolted upright
from shallow slumber.

The sound hove and sustained
as out of nightmare,

which she ran through cold to find him
sobbing, wound in quilt

clenched tight to chest. *What's
the matter, boy?* Her own voice

shaking. Some small poison
leaking through that room.

He told her of the snakes between
sob-chokes, while she rubbed

his back and sang low. *One of them
nightmares is all, Durant.*

Hain't a thing to fret about. But knew
her son was touched. Saw

the change in his face, skin
    translucent from horror,

a fever set hard in his eyes.
    She sat up with him, sang

and shushed him back to sleep
    until dawn's red broke dark.

3. The Snake Spells Plagued Him

The snake spells plagued him.
    Those first weeks, she tried

snakeroot hung from curtain
    rods. Pots of mint flanked

the sill. One night, Bledsoe
    lay himself in a tub of hot water

his father had drawn, closed
    his eyes, let water

sweep over mouth and nose
    as though he were dead–

hidden in the theory of loss lest
    he suffer more the yellow demon.

His mother caught him
    in that morbid stillness,

snatched him up and dried him.
    Relentless: the sixth week

found the snakeroot black
    and shrunken. The mint pots

fallen and shattered. She wept:
    He was marked. So it was

Vaney'd have to see him,
    high on the bald mountain,

young girl ditched by kin
    to live alone, red-blotched

face a pox to them, a family shame
    and proof of godlessness–

the girl who now survived by helping
    the sick beset with herb

and chant, ointment and recipe
    borne of earth and myth.

The girl would know, if anybody did,
    how to life and raze his hex.

4. On the Spine of the Ridge

On the spine of the ridge,
　　morning's moonlight blotted

elm and briar brush in its ruined
　　milk, haze of approaching rain.

Air tanged, sibilant. Farsighted,
　　struck through with revelation.

Autumn's machinations
　　raised the orchard's wine-scent,

each apple a womb of cloud,
　　each stem a deciduous trance

this high up, where the world
　　became a sealed mouth.

Steep grade, mountainside,
　　where thunder snarled down.

Wind heaved and flattened
　　in the valley. Shredded.

Up around the switchback,
　　mother and son leaned forward

headlong in rhododendron. Ascending
　　slow and deliberate in pre-dawn

blue to the cabin now opening
　　sheer on rock's edge, where

untamed hedges haloed the witch-den,
　　Vaney's one-room cabin

in shocks of green. One the porch,
rocking. Blonde hair visible,

froth spilled foaming over
her shoulders. Peach pit face

floated in the cornflower light,
legs mottled red

and bruise-dappled, pig hide
wrapped around her knees.

Smiled: teeth perfect and girlish,
a crescent flash, mica-bright.

He's a fine lookin' boy. Fine.
Why y'all come to Vaney?

Her voice a fiddle string gone
gothic and shrieking.

Shamed, fraught, his mother
cried the story.

5. I See He's a Special Child, Miss

I see he's a special child, Miss.
He hain't jumpy like most

boys, don't take to talk nor carryin' on.
But this hain't no effect

of any curse. Many youngerns'll
have snakes slither

up in their dreams. This'n is odd,
but I wouldn't carry on

about it. Let'm lay on a pallet in your
room, but don't block

the winder with a shawl. Let
the moon shine in, airish.

Lay the child on yonder
side of your bed so he don't

have a view to it. Hain't crucial,
but if it'll bring'm some ease,

hang you a bell or two 'round
the winder. Snakeroot

n' mint weren't the way to tend it.
Rub you some minty salve

on his chest and right up on his
nose, so he don't get

to thinkin' he smells their fumes
a-plumin' in the air.

6. She Asked to Speak to the Child

She asked to speak to the child
    alone. His mother withdrew,

yielding after Bledsoe
    nodded his head, took

a step forward. He paced slow up
    to the porch, dawnlight

now full gold. A sweet scent
    burnt on the girl,

pine-smoke and pear syrup.
    His mouth watering.

She culled him a pear-half
    and, as he chewed,

spoke low and frantic,
    conspiratorial, unheard

by his mother whose silhouette
    soaked deep in daylight,

down a ways on
    the slope. Vaney took hold

of his hand. He fixed on
    her hair, so not to gawk

on her ravaged features,
    deep pits and scars,

pearlescent thatches
    of cheek and cut lip–

Now you got to take count
of what I say, child.

I do not know what that
yeller snake means.

Could be a spirit come in
that smells somethin'

in you, it could mean
a ghost aimin' to

warn you of somethin' else.
I don't think it the angel

of death, but if it is, I don't
think it means to take you.

It's keen on somethin' else, somethin'
you cain't see nor smell

nor hear. So if you're tetched,
I hain't the one to tell you.

I know you and your mama
are afeared to come a-huntin'

all the way up'is hill. But I don't
have no answers. I do

know your mama has to think
them serpents can be purged.

Chances are they'll be by time
and prayer, but she's a might

worried. You can see dark in her
eyes, her bones raised sharp

in her cheeks, so you cain't test her
no more. Let her slumber.

Don't weep or holler out in
the night if you can

hep it. Don't climb up on the bed
twixt your daddy and her

and cling to 'em. Lay down on
that pallet behind their bed

long as you're afeared. And
if you feel that heaviness

press down on your chest,
keep your eyes shet,

ask your mama to let you
plug your ears up with cloth.

I wisht there was an herb or mix
that'd make them serpents

coil up and die,
but spirits will remain.

7. Grown Little, Nine-Years-Old, Bledsoe Upset

Grown little, nine-years-old, Bledsoe upset
in the mud-bloodied water with the preacher.

Congregation looking on with intense pity,
father absent with work and mother

with hands masking mouth. Knowing this violence
would bring him to grace. *He'll always be a child,*

the preacher had told her, *be we got to put him*
down in the water of Jesus anyhow. We got to make

sure he saved, what for that devil in his dream–
Snakes breathed all around them,

unseen: cottonmouths, copperheads,
timber rattlers. They writhed

into their lives, roiling, turgid. *We are here*
today, Lord, to see the dark defeated in this child.

We are here to heave the Spirit into him, that he might
swoon into Your love and wreck the viper

ruining him, unholy ghost that squirmed
right up into his soul! Amen

and hallelujah! The gathering now a dazed opera
of trills and moans, shouts and crescendos.

Women's cheeks gone rosy and hot,
men reaching violent to air.

So he was steeped down rough through that
unbreathable nimbus of light,

the world a shattered window exposing the dun
    storm of sin, where hands of clarity

caught the boy gasping, glacial. Again
    blubbering ablution, again down.

Nostrils and mouth washed choking, strangled
    glossolalia. Down brutal, forced into that flux

of signs and wonders, doxology lung-crammed.
    The preacher's sunburned hands

a tedious crown. The dead thrummed
    and twined right down through

the child's heart, scrubbing the mind immaculate.
    Wind purled with hymn, far from him

but earth-doused in the water
    where he'd always rise again.

8. In Those Slow Autumns

In those slow autumns, when Bledsoe
woke cured into the glow

of that new world, free of curse
or mark, still all but wordless,

he'd work and watch the mineral
shimmer of the hillside,

the crescent moon reap horizon's
distant tree-sway, thresh

floor and scythe, chipped,
hard-used. Gleaned.

Nights she'd brush his hair and sing
as he lay in her lap. Her voice

quartz-bright and deep, lyrics
hauling up that land and its

dimming myth. Nights, when moon
sliced overhead, his father

took him out and showed him stars
and planets, told him

that the Lord's house was so vast
that the glimmers they witnessed

were likely dead and dark now.
Time knits a blue fire,

sign that memory
long outshines the body.

9. Harvest Paradox, Autumn's Pilfer

Harvest paradox, autumn's pilfer:
    An apple pitched to earth's

swell, a squint in black-eyed grass,
    the church where worms bore

votive hunger, stripped
    the mortal body,

cleansed to sate the gut and heart.
    Dawn slanted on the tip

of late October and ripped fog
    apart, apples a scumble

of juice the keen wasps thrashed,
    wings lodged in flesh.

Ants scalded, flushed out all
    divisible. Their tiny fires

swarmed, smoked. Even rot
    absolved. Seeds let loose

and buoyant on the mas
    of their own beginning,

all marked by
    what it lacked.

10. Pulp of Dying Mountain Town, Its Remnant

Pulp of dying mountain town, its remnant
    rust-works, railway and mining deaths

cached by mycotrophic vines and barbed wire
    twining the pits, Blue Ridge pottery

toothed in clay. Wind a gasp of sorrel
    and stagnancy. Mountains: towering

monasteries of doubt. Chore of hog-slay,
    smack of ax head and helve,

disemboweling of liver, lights. Brains,
    gray corymbs scooped from skull.

Killed to live: killed after the blackberries,
    killed after the oak bore the blood-leaf's

prophecy, after winter's first frost.
    What was spring here but empty

remedy? Valley farm like a collapsed body.
    Here and there stands of winter oak.

Everywhere contagion that seethed
    up through sagged porches and musty

bedrooms blackening in corners. Resin-leaks.
    A mattress thin on box-springs, quilt

under a cross to assure that spirit forsook
    the body. Kept minds locked tight

in the heartwood of myth. And Bledsoe's
    sleep deep without a pillow.

Beaten down into dream: The house
    filled up like a creek bed root-choked,

the rooms spat out and left to fester.
    Where could a man run off to solitude,

break out of cellar-smother, air cached in
    jarred jelly and pipe-water: Past

pared to summary?

II. Let Him Be Shut of Us, Lord

Let him be shut of us, Lord
he heard her say

of his father, now tucked
tight in afghans, counterpane.

Lord, let him go.
Nightstand crowded

with salves and pills,
whiskey with lemon

and rosemary for what
they called the brain-burn,

meningitis gnawing
from the outside in–

one week he was smiling
with Bledsoe, a farm tutor

teaching him seeding seasons
and the endless betrayal

of rain, how to fight back
in the planting, soothe

husk-dry hills. Renegade
summers burned crops

to dust. And little things:
Apple flesh, corn

tasseling, arrowheads
and toad-holes. Squirrel

hunt and cleaning, the pungent
stew, fried potatoes, pears,

coffee with sugar and cream.
Then, his spirit simply settled

into a chair to rock constantly,
as paralysis clamped down

that need for movement,
even as the muscles locked

in confusion. He found a window
into himself, a silent

and fettered place
that allowed no talk

or trespass in the observable
world, now vanished.

And when mornings
staked their claim,

the fat sun like a headlight
breaking over the valley,

he groaned and barked
at the light Bledsoe

and mother had to souse
with anything that could

blind the windows:
cardboard, foil, old

sheets they used to line
the dog kennel.

Lord, let him be shut of us,
that he might be freed

into your mercy. Let his ghost
rise up to fix on you.

Bledsoe sat at bedside,
his father trying to catch

onto a word he could
not utter, eyewhites yellow,

bloodrimmed. Panicked
in the too-bright blackness.

Now the narrative stalled forever.
Now past and future dovetailed

into that room, Bledsoe's
heart pitted, cored clean.

12. He Walked Lonesome

He walked lonesome,
    turned in on himself,

a storm-slaked petal.
    Scalp stung cold.

Memory's wound,
    marled heart.

Sloped north to woods,
    away from the place

they buried his father.
    Only proof

of his life the gray days
    of the farm collapsing.

Mound of dirt: father's
    shabby means to rapture.

13. His Father

His father who brought
him melon candy.

Who confided. Who loved
so much the creek

rocks and minnows, treefrogs
and milkweed, who helped

the future tether its green.
Whose warmth now

doused. Who entered
the final door. Whose

likeness faded fast as November's
sun, lantern snuffed.

Now to crave a story.
Only the hickory's wind

rasped him a song,
the tale clipped just under

the blossom of clarity.
No bond or union.

Scattered, stoic. Curt.
Needed someone

to grant him a reason
beyond a beginning

and end, to gift some
country logic for all

this dark. Where were
the storytellers here?

The trees stood blank
and swaying like tongue-

tied mill workers in the Holmes
General Store, bodies gone

slack from abuse or sheer
fatigue. Sick or crippled,

silent in their turn.
All bracken and tobacco,

dirty jokes or long looks
on the lack of rain–

a rumor built hollow
on drought and waterline.

Mostly wordless, hot glares
homeward, where dishes

crashed, shattered from frustration.
Pent-up rage cordoned

off in women suppressed
by propriety, gossiped

into silence that set their
hearts dark, wrecked.

14. Unlike His Father, Some Men

Unlike his father, some men
    in these hills did not know

how to react in the face
    of ultimate circumstance.

Like lightning, in their mad
    climb up from the ground,

they rushed to marry whatever
    descended. Desperation creates

a sound, a hum that haunts
    them like childhood

hymns borne clutched
    of Old Testament fear,

hum like a blind primeval
    fish droning beneath

an ocean storm. They settled
    for eaves slanting the sky

down to a cistern clattering
    with whatever the sky conferred.

15. In Years He Mended, Dusks

In years he mended, dusks
    a blue smolder of memory:

His father faded behind
    the creak of the barn door,

mouth trembling with
    sermons lodged timeless

behind his tongue, warnings
    Bledsoe kept hidden,

sacrosanct in the snare
    of that house. He breathed

dust and drank the well's
    rust-water, slogged in

the heat of horses, saddled
    by noon rains, mud choking

the yield. Nights, back in
    the stanch purity of those

rooms, with soap-burned
    hands he wrapped his head

with words: *sorghum* and *lantern,*
    cellar and *sin.* Then down

into image, the earth's nightlong
    gift: His father's scarred hands

fondling the plump coinage
    of tomatoes, pox of aphids

washed immaculate. His gloves
    uncoiling barbed wire, gauzing

the reddening scrape. Hiss
    and warmth of embers,

cedar smoke's tang. Always
    his father dimmed again

under black water as mornings
    wrested him from sleep

like a breech foal torn loose,
    shivering in the hay.

16. Carry Me to the Doctor, Boy

Carry me to the doctor, boy,
she said, the pain in her

face a puzzle of lines: *Take me*
off this hill and down to the clinic.

She had started with the sick
headaches, compresses,

nausea and joint-pain, for weeks
sleepless and down.

He carried her piggyback,
past barns and shells of farms

long rotten, repossessed
by horse bones and rusted

grates. An earth that wouldn't give.
Then down Central Street

where the cold was more
than wind, where drivers

slowed to gawk, the man-child
with mother heaved up on

his back, bounded in unwashed
quilts. His brow a red crag

of worry. Her weight bearing down
on his neck–pain and stifle,

the heft like a sin no prayer
would erase, ghost-leech.

Spine a line of ache. Blood
pumping flush crimson

and blistering in his eyes,
sight gone sun-blotched

and lungs winded, molars
clenched tight and ground.

Into the doctor's
swung-door air of Lysol mist,

medicinal cold. Old women
under wreathes of blue-rinse

hair scooted away, slanted
their mouths in disgust:

Grease and mothball smells
clung to her, to him like gauze.

Let me set, and she stared
ahead unwavering, ignorant

decorum flat on her features until
the sun crept arthritic through

the sole window and cast
its limb-shadowed light

on his cheek. They called her
back to those white halls.

17. He Chose Silence

He chose silence in that
    simple light, cooling

in the room of judgement,
    those eyes flickering

at him, back and forth
    in wordless gossip:

That's the man-boy doesn't
    speak. That's his Mama

what came in like a sack
    of sticks on his shoulders.

Looked into himself:
    Recollection crammed

like a closet overflowing–
    some soft treasure lost

down in that dark and dust,
    down in the dank nooks

where a fire burned without
    light or heat, like a snake

roped hot into calm, the eyes
    shimmered alive, emeralds.

18. Heart-Pound, Blood-Rush

Heart-pound, blood-rush,
    memories of boneset

and bloodroot snapped off
    on field's edge and brought

to her in those days the kitchen
    sang with crackles, steam.

Vegetables burbled plump
    in the boil. She lay his gift

in a tall blue glass. The red
    roots turned to fade

in the water, groundless
    but shocked alert.

19. What They Told Me

What they told me is I don't
have long. Something's grown

in my head and spread 'round
to other parts. They want

to coop me up in a hospital
up yonder in Knoxville.

I told'em I'd die at home. I won't
have my spirit trapped up

in a strange city. He hauled her
on his back after he got

the shawl on her shoulders.
She clasped her arms

tight around his throat. *You goin'*
to have to take me round to Crane's

so I can get them pills. He'll put it
on our tab. lord knows I hain't

got the money to pay'm nohow.
Swung door back into heat

of the day, the sun high
and bright. He stared

ahead, blood pounding fierce
in his forehead. Swallowed.

I hain't goin' back to no doctor.
I told'em you'd look after me.

After the pharmacy, he'd take
    one of two trails back home:

the first sheer, the second
    briar-strewn, neither easy.

20. In Middle Age, in Those First Leaf-strains

In middle age, in those first leaf-strains
  and the smoke-tinct of winter, in the birdless day,

the memory becomes augural.
  An unearthed gospel, the story ends

before it begins, tale in fragments and strewn
  like shards at a man's feet. This fact

forced Bledsoe to tread north till small hills
  angled up and the pond on their land's rim

came to view. The church on its west end,
  hollow and crumbling on a berm of weeds.

Ain't supposed to be up here in the gloaming
  He moved on anyway. Stripped his clothes

and walked into the water-grass, waded
  across to the cold center. Shivered.

Ain't supposed to be up here in this water
  this time of day. Daddy said it was deeper'n most.

He'd imagined a train car lodged beneath
  the surface, red, rusting, and lined with

bones of the trapped. Dreamed of gold
  treasure flashing down in the water weeds,

pearl strings and fish eggs stippling the mud.
  And the farm tools of his great-grandfather,

chaff-cutter and flail, scythe and breast ploughs
  half hidden in a century of rain.

Congregated, washed to fracture. His feet
    dangling over a universe forgotten. Ancientry.

Suddenly, he knew: knew by autumn cirrus bluing
    in the dark. By the wind-tip spilling a chill

on pine, cones plopping into shallows,
    the gar beneath him shocked from his frigid

heaven of muck. Water moccasins dragging
    the black pennants of their bodies beneath

the shale. And in dead center, him, a chalk god
    noctilucent in the violet air, who knew

the pond had become prayer, somewhere beyond throat
    and brain, beyond tongue and voice–

21. Dear God of the Dead-haunted

Dear God of the dead-haunted
heart, this water streams

with night and stars. My mind
a tinderbox, set to flare

from the fire your voice conveys.
Faith a wooden pendulum–

this surface a door that gathers
to take me in. God of my kin

and bindweed bloom, glacier
and chert, light darkens

withing her, back there in
the overrun meadow, back

there in the house where I was
born. My mind is the field

where cattle ribs inherit
earth, stripped by vultures

and rain, where that house
slants down into soil

My body a shadowbox,
a grave of silt. An aging

pine sheathed in resin,
leaning away from the source

that helped it begin. Swarmed
with buried incident. Piled

the days, gnawed them back,
whittled down by those failed

purgations of grief. And no words
left but the words I remember:

one is farewell. *And though*
loneliness sits on my eyelids

nightly, I know at least that the earth
will remember me, this body

your decoding of stone, star, nebula,
the axle of the moon locked,

this world a kingdom of weeds.
The horizon shimmers, the tipped

strata of leaf-sway, cloud, and question–
God, seeped in cells of wind-

fall apples, bee-burrows
drunk on the hymns

of excess, singing the hours
to barns and fences, singing

the sweet smoke above
the tree line, far-distant,

hedged by the cold wind
that descends to greet it,

God, have I only to tarry
here? Have I to turn

with the earth bearing little
more than the pure

knowledge of the unborn,
my voice sewn shut, burned

by this valley? If water
were death's kingdom,

if this small, off-set yawn
of pond the way to drown

down into paradise,
then help me break

though the worms' domain.
Let my shadow enter.

22. Nights He Moseyed through the House

Nights he moseyed through the house
    and heard her mumble in sleep–

somewhere wrapped like a carcass
    in that foul bed, acting out

on the floor. Mumbles to moans, and he
    was shocked to see her stumble

through the bedroom, pounding on walls,
    where the cloud-shadows threw spirits

on the headboard's Christ in his fossilized
    agony, manifest witness.

And there, up near the window, a slack
    board where the snow-cold seeped in,

making the skin itch like fire, the eyes water
    as though swathed with sumac, the hair

brittle like the stems of char-dry
    trillium on the sill. His father gone,

Bledsoe saw how the tiles uncaulked. Walls
    gave way to stud and ragged pine,

plumbing spilling its rusty bones. He knew
    nothing of hammer or washer, chisel or saw:

The faucet ticked on like a tally, reckoning
    the days Bledsoe struggled to cultivate

the world his father began, a force
    uncontainable, too wild to tame.

23. No Sheets, His Head

No sheets, his head
    a sweaty node pressed

down and jerking
    on the pallet, teeth

grinding hard to
    cause pain he suffers

even in dream, Bledsoe's
    tracked by dog-wolves

gone fanatical with rage,
    their faces torn into

rags, their mouths
    all black and sneer.

He staggers up winded
    to the corn plot;

the one ember of that
    far house's window

dims, turns him away.
    The east woods, the only

good timber, on fire,
    the whole ridge roaring

up to veil the stars
    in smoke. Spreading

toward the orchard. The wind
    epiphanic in its bluster.

And among the corn, bodies
    blackened and propped

up, standing scorch-still, their
    arms outstretched as though

petrified in a search for someone,
    something to embrace, to take

with them. And voices. Jumbled,
    codified whimpers and groans

the only evidence of their plight.
    The beasts race past them

and scatter their bodies to dust.
    The voices go on, dark amulets

of sound, when the world slants to a series
    of steep berms and moon-flickered

ditches. Land's furrows stone-choked,
    pocks over which he stumbles, death's

hounding frigid at his nape.
    He can see them now, their teeth

black and grating. Snouts wild, bloody
    in the starlight. He knows their fur

mats with blood of their kills. Knows
    their purpose chills them to shivering

even as their hearts thrash triple-time,
    eyes raking the pines where he now

hides, where their bodies lunge as wind
    reveals him, the moon's cold tooth to bite.

24. Found His Father's Rum Jug

Found his father's rum jug
  under the floor boards

and drank deep and slapdash
  until rivulets plashed ground

and he stumbled forth
  in his grief. His mother

screaming. Staggered in delirium.
  Conjured images would

scrub the pain: A thousand
  blue-chalk moths collapsing

the fence, a blood-red moon
  dousing the grass as he laughed,

looking for a passage or a stable.
  He kept his head cocked

to the purple staghorn leaf,
  moss's buried sound. Stars

spinning. Thought he sensed
  the underground runnels

sluice to bloom the hearts
  of every seed, bulb. Whatever

song he heard in the wind's
  clatter sunk his ear back

to silence, that drawn-out
  syllable, that gaping vowel

of his mother's mouth sprouting
    a brown rose behind him.

He couldn't move his tongue
    now: Had no hymns.

Leaf-swarmed, he lay down in
    the boggy paddock.

Night cradling him in the fetid
    mess of his burden.

25. Once, When He Woke Before Dawn

Once, when he woke before dawn,
  Bledsoe went to check on her,

sat at the fireplace drawn down
  to a knot of ash. No wind,

and rain a memory, gothic underglow
  in the day's gray hand. Then a red shimmer

at the window caught in his periphery,
  then red-green flash and hum–

a hummingbird. Flirting with the scaffolding
  and panes, its ruby throat flush

with life. Walked into the yard, air a weird
  warm. And yonder, the backyard's oak

a vast red brain of hummingbirds merged
  in nodal fluttering and iridescence,

awake. Sky dark yellow and no wind,
  like moments before disaster. Dogs whined

in the north, bayed frantic, raspy tremolo.
  Dizzy, he stumbled back indoors, closed

                the door, bolted lock and chain.

26. Death of an Orchard

Death of an orchard: Deserted
    under the farm's harsh spillage

of sunlight, parts of apples
    tumbled to ground where even

grass turned away: Inside
    them, the cold pulse pushed

between roots and dust. Rain
    couldn't unhinge cores choked

with weed-wire, the day leaking
    through and hardening to shards.

27. Spring Came, Winged Seeds

Spring came, winged seeds
    lifted to sun. Skeletal radiance

of the land's Pentecostal
    light. Warmth for weeks

prepared the oak limbs, so deep
    life shimmered in their jagged

matrix, sky-blue grosbeak eggs,
    the fattened meat of squirrels.

Winter's flawless knife sliced
    a wound that wouldn't bleed

land until summer's force
    leaned hard on the flesh

of the farms, furrowed
    rows of melon and corn.

Bledsoe walked through
    Kendal's orchard, down hills

west to town. Skimmed the beech
    trees, their char-dark trunks

a puzzle solved by afternoon's
    cumuli–moving fast and low

eastward. *Mama said a loaf*
    of bread, a jar of minty salve, aspirin.

He mouthed the command
    every few minutes, below

whisper, head leaned
    forward in worried intent.

Kept the dollar bills
    she gave him clinched sweaty

in his left palm, balled up
    tight lest he lose them to the weeds.

28. To Wash Her. Up in the Dank Room, Her Body

To wash her. Up in the dank room, her body
    sketched in heat. He brought the sponge

and scalding soap-water, woke her, helped
    her sit on the bed's edge. Wheezing. Face

mostly teeth and pits. Pain with every heartbeat.
    He gently touched her face. Smells of sweat

and sweet rot. Body giving way to bone. Blood on bed,
    midway down. *Time to warsh, Durant?*

I 'spec it is, boy. Wait that I catch my breath. An' go fetch
    us a clean washcloth along with that sponge.

Outside, strict downwardness–rain pelted the bent
    grass, black branch flickered in the flash.

His mother bone-cold, bone-fevered
    in her own generous storm,

sea-surge of atoms fast to seep
    organs with waste. Earth's dark talent,

body's cells in aspiration. To wash her. After he
    rinsed her neck and back and tucked her again

into her ache, the post-rain creek raged
    with flux, called birds to tentative praise–

Thus her body's din attuned with April trees,
    dread lit by her mind that softly turned to song.

29. She Slept in Fits and Fever

She slept in fits and fever
with an eerie smile,

convinced down deep in
the white-hot realm

of ill-fed delusion
that two gray faces

of the sparrow lived
among her kin.

Sparrow east, sparrow
west. *Most times birds,*

but sometimes they's old
women. Old and wiry

and hacking up dust. Lord,
but kind. They'd a-brung me

anything: firewood, good
'maters in the dead

of February, a killed, cleaned
deer. They'd a-brung me

the moon if I'd asked.
Her mind an attic

where the chimney passed
through. Where dust,

ash, and sparrows
settled hard and nodal

in the corpus callosum.
Lord I 'member one time

my daddy got up, hollered
and blasted them possums

plum from the porch in dark
morning. When I woke

to the yard I saw that kyarn
hard and unashamed

in the first sun. The ol' farm mutt
nursed a maggot-hole deep

as an eye socket in the bulged
back of the biggest'un

Like a little bone-thatched cove.
Like a grin a-blood. We didn't

et the meat, though we needed it.
And I 'member that little box

of churchlight yonder where
Durant and I'd a-sing

in tongues. He'd get afeared
and I'd have to stop half

through the spell and fetch him
home. He'd be a-weepin'

constant. Memory's door gave
way to worse fever, heat

like a open oven. *Oh, Lord,*
there's them sparrows in

the basement. She convulsed in
her vision of ash-gray birds

preening in the cellar's
    vegetable dark, mold

like religion spreading
    into the least cranny,

deep into wooden joists,
    up through rust-grazed

pipework and yellow
    rat bones, walls' relics.

Lord, them two sparrows'll be
    anywhere I want'em.

Sisters under my own skin.
    Her forehead gushing.

Mouth dry, a socket. Eyes
    squinting into a light

that wasn't there. *I 'spec*
    I need y'all to bring me

some water and a rag
    to wet my eyes. The roof

above her now cloud,
    letting in wind and rain.

30. Then the World to Black

Then the world to black.
    She still dreamed of green

lawns, minnows, hickory-horned
    devil moths. But dark rings

around the pictures: A haze of gnats
    rimmed the woods, goats and rye

on the wind. Winter rolled on
      to flower, a sweep of bright

cells. No matter: The field
      shrieked into grief. Hour

of thorns, the stone cutter's
    chisel. Go ahead and let the world

                        return to dust.

31. Time to Leave You

Time to leave you, boy. I'd suture you to me
if I could. Closed her eyes: Cancer

crawled in her like spiderlings
hatched from withered sacs

of her lungs. Walked wincing.
From her bed the salve-smell

sweat on sheets: always around
him. The ache, always: She begged

and begged, nightly now–
Boy, all I ask is a smother

in my sleep Curl up some hemlock
in my tea. Out. He needing

out from the blunt weight of her smock
as she sat at dinner, forking

the bread, eating nothing. *Durant,*
you hain't got no sense to know I suffer.

You hain't got a mind to do nothing.
Land's feculence suffocating him

in its shoveled-over residue. Her breath
like leaf-rot, apples set to blister in

the August sear. Take no mind
of the molder. Turn your head away.

32. In the Keening House, in the Night's Arc

In the keening house, in the night's arc
    over her coughing fits and pleadings,

he stargazes from his pallet.
    A rush of living dark tears through

the country air, through the tall grasses,
    shakes loose over his sternum. To share

the panic of fleeing creatures–
    The awful fact of leaving her

dead and cooling in the house. No matter
    how far his flight, her body would mound

under quilts, her flesh would swell
    blue in the room whorled with stench.

So with the flick of a flame,
                        there it would go.

33. Went

Went. Cross-beams
    seethed and cracked

the end. The farm's
    old bones unlatched

a tall blaze, dawn behind
    a cloud of gasoline.

34. Dusk Comes, Heat Stays, Still

Dusk comes, heat stays, still
    douses his hair in salt, sweat.

Lost, lulled by dark, Bledsoe misreads
    the far hound's yowl as lullaby.

He limps on down to the stream
    bank, briar lashes needling

chiggers on his skin. Down further
    to the tick-leafed, scallop-prongs

of the sand-slews, rushes and snarl
    of water full of musk-smell,

cottonmouths folding their bodies
    deeper under, spring's bulls

and peepers terror-plopping.
    He washes scalp, face,

blood and cinder away and gone.
    Then, cooled, props his head

against the berm and bonders on
    her teeth, gnashed in

the death-frown, her eyes astonished
    and rolled-back white.

Bites down gently on his tongue,
                                        sleeps.

35. A Blackness Amplified, Greenness Insinuated

A blackness amplified, greenness insinuated:
    Insects chisel the night to a point. Summer

clouds bear no star. Beyond the tangle of limbs
    and detritus of a thousand falls, out east

toward the farms and the clearing, the house
    lies in a pile of smolder. What seeps

into the brain's dark apertures? What ignites
    the night's grammar or douses it silent,

something sheer and simple, quartz-glow?
    Sepal-green, the earth's rejuvenating

pain. Suddenly, a man lies down
    in his guilt and asks: Are you the lattice

or the bloom? Answers come as platitudes,
    tricks of dead light, peripheral. Thus sleep

forces signs, trespass, yellow dust in the throat.
    Summer turns quick yet heavy-footed,

more potent than the fever
    that bleeds through him like a flower.

36. Something Deep in Bledsoe's Vitals

Something deep in Bledsoe's vitals
    strikes violent, itch turned pain

turned mania, clot in neck-vein
    and thalamus twinge. Heat holiness.

Body slumps, simply still
    in the climbing scald of morning.

37. They Find Him Near Noon

They find him near noon,
  the law's dogs set crazed on his reek.

Even as they haul him away,
  looking for the right cage for him

to wither in, his mind lies
  distant, radiant. Trees blossom,

lean away, give him
  room. Eyes scoured, his face

calcified, a coin set gleaming
  in the closing vault of days.

Acknowledgments

I thank James Clinton Howell and Brandon Wicks, friends who commented on the manuscript in earlier drafts; their insights and meticulous eyes helped sculpt *Bledsoe* into its present form. Second, I thank Paul Ruffin, who published the short version of *Bledsoe* (comprised of sections 1 and 31 through 37) in *The Texas Review*. I appreciate him nominating the poem for a Pushcart Prize; his enthusiasm for the shorter version of the poem emboldened me to create this book-length version. I thank all Appalachian poets, particularly those who appear in *The Southern Poetry Anthology, Volume III: Contemporary Appalachia*. These radiant works inspired many details of *Bledsoe's* setting, character, and tone. Finally, I thank my writer friends, especially Dan Morris, Jesse Graves, and again James Clinton Howell and Brandon Wicks, whose conversation, fraternity, and support never fail to encourage and vivify.

About the Author

WILLIAM WRIGHT is author or editor of over twenty nationally published books, with several forthcoming. Most recently, Wright published *Grass Chapels: New & Selected Poems* with Mercer University Press in 2021. Wright has been named the Georgia Author of the Year, the Georgia Editor of the Year, and won the Terrain.org Grand Prize. Wright was named Writer-in-Residence at the University of Tennessee in 2016 and Visiting Assistant Professor of English and Creative Writing at Emory University and Oxford College of Emory from 2017-2020. Currently, he's working on a novel, a collection of essays, and a volume of poetry.